Ambition's Not An Awful Word

Author: Zack Zage   Illustrator: Adam Watkins

zackzage@gmail.com   adamfwatkins@hotmail.com

Copyright © 2012 by Ivy Court Press, LLC.

Published by Ivy Court Press, LLC. in Williamsburg, Virginia

Library of Congress Control Number: 2011933888

ISBN: 978-0-9836078-2-3

Printed in the United States of America

www.ivycourtpress.com

Ambition's Not An Awful Word

Written by Zack Zage

Illustrated by Adam Watkins

'Twas early in the school year, my teacher had a plan.
"'Me bags' were our first grade gig. Grade two we mailed Flat Stan.
Third grade was filled with haiku poems. Now that's my cup of tea.
This year, dear class, the theme for you is, 'what I want to be.'"

My hand shot up. "Me first! Me first!" Ms. Grundy stared me down.
"We'll start with Ann A. She'll go first. Zack, don't act like a clown."
Oh no, that dreaded alphabet. Why was my last name Zage?
But with the bell about to ring, I finally took the stage.

"If I were an astronaut, I'd rocket to the moon,
Gobble blobs of blue green cheese with mom's spatula spoon.
I would fill up Mare Tranquility with purple jello mix,
Play soccer with Andromeda or Hale-Bopp just for kicks."

"But," the moon would say, "Keep your hands to yourself.
Put your head on your pillow. Leave that spoon on the shelf.
If you fiddle with the Universe or just the Milky Way,
You could turn Polaris on her head and screw up night and day."

"If I were a cowpoke with a ten gallon hat,
I'd ride a dozen Brahma bulls in three seconds flat.
I'd wrastle longhorn steer with one arm behind my back.
I'd ride 'Bodacious' blindfolded, without any tack."

"Here's a pitchfork, pardner, and the keys to my truck.
Now get back to the barn. Finish cleaning up the muck.
Throw some scratch to the chickens. And fix that ol' leak.
'Cause you won't see the front side of a pony this week."

"If I were a singer, I would sing before the Queen,
Be the best basso profundo, this world has ever seen.
I would sing like Luciano at the Cinderella Ball.
I would sing a cappella, at Carnegie Hall."

"But you are not a singer. You can't even hold a tune.
Your C sounds like a G. You may screech but you don't croon.
If you yodeled in a barn, all the cows and sheep would jeer.
Please get back in that shower, where no one else can hear."

"If I were a chef, Cordon Bleu at Versailles,
I'd wear a white tuxedo, cummerbund, and bow tie.
I would sauté like a maestro. My soufflé would be premier.
Julia Child would be my mentor. And I would have no peer."

But the stove would yell out, "STOP! Don't put that oil in there.
YOU still have a chance to run, but I won't have a prayer.
Tell the truth, you can't boil water, or make a piece of toast.
Go outside. Light a fire. Have yourself a weenie roast."

"If I were an artist, the critics all would flip.
The bigs at New York's MoMA would cry, 'This guy's really hip.'
From musicians by Picasso and the night skies of Van Gogh,
to Da Vinci's Mona Lisa, and ME, a one man show."

"Oh, your canvas is no Pollock. It is just a muddy mess.
Our teacher, Mrs. Grundy, thinks it's awful, more or less.
You had better stick with fingerpaint, rubber stamps, and glue.
'Cause all that junk that you call art is really double doo."

"If I were a doctor, I would free the world from pain.
Prescriptions would be candy. No illness would remain.
My magic glue would seal a cut without the slightest moan.
A touch here, a tweak there, would mend a broken bone."

"But you're a hypochondriac. This goal seems out of place.
The problem is the sight of blood could put you on your face.
You still cry 'MOM! I got boo boo', just 'cause your knee is sore.
If you were my physician, I'd be headed out the door."

"If I were an architect, my buildings all would soar.
The Eiffel Tower and Parthenon would be forgotten lore.
Beside the River Seine, sprawls my newest Taj Mahal.
From Montreal to Houston snakes my next China Wall."

"Well, Lego blocks and playing cards make great little toys.
But concrete, steel, and bricks are used by all us BIG boys.
You can build your castles in the sky or somewhere on a beach.
Kid, here's some good advice for you, 'Your grasp exceeds your reach.'"

"If I were a banker, I would wear a pinstrip suit.
I'd meet with lots of rich folks and deposit all their loot.
My address would be on Wall Street with a corner office view.
Oh, don't forget that bonus check. It's way overdue."

But, "NO!" protest the stockholders, "You're wasting all our cash!
Don't pocket all the goodies and leave us with the trash.
Nobody will invest here. They'll keep their dough in jars.
We'll fit you in a different stripe. Your new view – steel bars."

"If I were a lawyer, I'd be famous far and wide.
Undaunted on defense with Perry Mason by my side.
I would take a seat in Congress and legislate you healthy.
Then I'd head a DC lobby, and make myself wealthy."

"You can fool the people sometimes, but justice should be blind.
And the people at the ballot box are hardly ever kind.
When self-interest comes a'calling and you wallow in the mire,
We will topple that old soapbox, put your feet to the fire."

"If I were a writer, fans would rave, 'He's number one!'
The New York Times would ink: 'That Zage can really spin a pun.'
Quick columnists would crow, 'He is Billy Shakespeare's heir.
Only Austen, Dickens, Hugo, Joyce, and Poe can compare.'"

"But remember Mrs. Grundy? She might just disagree.
'I think he scored a zero on his last spelling bee.'
To the pundits, please explain the universe in which you dwell.
'Cause rhyming hat and cat won't make you Theodor Geisel."

Tough teens taunt, "You exaggerate. You're nothing but a boast.
It's always YOU who have to be the brightest and the most.
So, until the things you do, can back up the things you say,
The rest of us won't stick around and listen to you bray."

When my mom tucked me in last night she said, "Why feel so down?
Ambition's not an awful word. Wipe off that silly frown.
In your own imagination, you're supposed to reign supreme.
Oh, the moon left you this message, 'It's OK to dream.'"

Glossary

a cappella – The literal meaning of this Latin term is, "in the style of the chapel." Here, it means singing by myself.

ambition – A sincere desire to achieve, combining confidence, determination, and motivation.

Andromeda – A princess in Greek mythology, saved from a sea monster by Perseus, her future husband. This name in turn was given to a galaxy as well as a constellation which includes this galaxy.

Austen – (1775-1817) Jane was the British novelist who wrote: *Pride and Prejudice, Sense and Sensibility, Persuasion, Emma...*

basso profundo – The lowest male bass singing voice. Coloratura soprano is the highest female singing voice.

bigs – Bigwigs, VIPs, hotshots, experts, arbiters in the adjudication of what is art and what is not.

Billy Shakespeare – The nickname given to William Shakespeare by his closest friends.

Bodacious – A notorious bucking bull. Where cowboys fear to tread.

bonus check – An unexpected or, more recently, required payment to an executive employee as part of that employee's compensation.

boo boo – An owee, an ouchee. These terms were coined in the 1980s, when it became politically incorrect for an intelligent parent to use the term "scratch" when speaking with a child. Other banned words include: abrasion, bruise, cut, gash, laceration, scrape, sore...

bow tie – A tie in the shape of a hair bow worn around the neck, usually with a tuxedo. When I was a boy scout, we could have, theoretically, untied one and used it as a tourniquet. I am not certain why one might require a tourniquet at a formal gathering.

bray – The noise made by a mule, a donkey, or a kid (and not just the "kid'll eat ivy too" kind).

C and G – The former is a name I call myself, the latter, a drink with jam and bread. Also notes on the musical scale ABCDEFG.

canvas – A hip way to say painting.

Carnegie Hall – One of the premier concert halls in the United States. It is located in New York City.

China Wall – *The Great Wall of China*, one of the seven man made wonders. It took over 2,000 years to build and stretches over 3,500 miles.

Cordon Bleu – One of the finest cooking schools in the world. It originated in France in the 16th century. The name has become synonymous with a restaurant that serves food in this style.

croon – The noise made by Bing Crosby.

cummerbund – A wide cloth waistband worn in place of a vest. It is supposed to catch the food that falls out of your mouth before it stains your shirt. My mom used to make me wear a bib for this same purpose.

D C lobby – In Ulysses S. Grant's time, influence peddlers used to hang out in the bars and lobbies of Washington, DC hotels trying to curry favor with the legislators who frequented them. It is an organization with the sole purpose of swaying members of Congress, in any way possible, to vote for legislation that benefits that organization's client and against legislation that is not in that organization's client's best interest. People in these organizations make a lot of moolah. Many of them are ex-Congress members.

Da Vinci – (1452-1519) Leonardo was an Italian painter, inventor, and original "Renaissance man". He painted, *The Last Supper, The Adoration of the Magi, The Mona Lisa...*

deposit – This is something you do with money when you are not spending it.

Dickens – (1812-1870) Charles was the British novelist who wrote, *A Christmas Carol, A Tale of Two Cities, Bleak House, David Copperfield...*

different stripe – This refers to the horizontal stripe usually worn by the incarcerated.

double doo – A colloquial expression having something to do with the by-product of alimentation.

dough – Money, cash, loot, moolah, greenbacks, l'argent, dinero...a mixture of flour and water.

dreaded alphabet – This always seems to work against you in school. When you are prepared, you are never called on. When you are not, you are sure to be called on first.

Eiffel Tower – The tallest habitable structure in France. It was designed by Gustave Eiffel and completed in time for the 1889 World's Fair.

Flat Stanley – In the second grade, children mail cardboard "Stanleys" all over the world. The receiver takes a photo with Stanley and, for instance, Machu Picchu or the Hindu Kush in the background and then mails it back to the kid, who shows it to the class.

forgotten lore – All of the history, knowledge, and beliefs that are no longer remembered. There is a lot of forgotten lore on high school and college campuses.

gig – A colloquial expression meaning a job. My brother had a gig playing the drums. My other brother used to gig frogs and flounder before he accidentally gigged me and dad took the gig away from him.

goodies – Benefits resulting from hard work or investments, cookies and candy.

grasp exceeds your reach – Under normal circumstances, you cannot grasp anything that exceeds your reach – but you can dream.

haiku – A poem, seventeen syllables, three lines, 5-7-5, repeat after me.

Hale-Bopp – The brightest comet, to earthlings, in the 20th century. Fortunately, for Boston College, Mary and not Bopp was there to assist when Doug Flutie passed the football to Gerard Phelen on the last play of the game against Miami in November of 1984.

heir – A survivor who gets the dough when someone dies. This is, unfortunately another gift to posterity from Henry XVIII. (see was / were) Everyone knows Henry had a slight speech impediment. He could not pronounce the letters H or K. To this very day, we don't either when we use words like heir, herb, knot, know, and knight. Lucky for us, muc of wat ing enry ad to offer to umanity is lost. E was illed by a night and fell ead over eels off is orse. Lucky for them, both his pet nat and his pet nu survived.

hip – Something that is replaced along with a knee after, no, no in this usage it means really cool, keen, neat, swell, groovy, smashing...

hold a tune – An idiomatic expression meaning to have the ability to sing a song in tune.

hypochondriac – A term used to describe someone who is unwell or believes they are.

Hugo – (1802-1885) Victor was the French novelist who wrote, *Les Miserables, The Hunchback of Notre Dame...*

invest – To put money or capital into a business or a government with the expectation (unfortunately, sometimes false expectation) of removing more than you put in at some later date.

jars – In the depression of the1930s, after the banks failed (see invest), some people buried their money in Mason jars in their backyard. They may still do it.

jeer – The noise made by Philadelphia sports fans.

Joyce – (1882-1941) James was the Irish novelist who wrote, *Ulysses, A Portrait of the Artist as a Young Man, Finnegans Wake...*

Julia Child – (1912-2004) The preeminent American chef and author of the best selling cookbook, *Mastering the Art of French Cooking.*

justice is blind – "Lady Justice" is depicted carrying a sword in one hand and a set of scales in the other. She is wearing a blindfold. This metaphor implies that any fair judicial system should not be based on observable traits (beauty, personal finances, connections...) This is not to be confused with your feelings about a referee with whom you have a disagreement.

legislate you healthy – This is when Congress passes laws that protect you from yourself. It's a wonder humans were able to survive that first few million years without the help of Congress.

loot – Money, dollars, cash, moolah, dough...

Luciano – (1935-2007) Pavarotti was one of the "Three Tenors" and the most famous male operatic singer of the 20th Century.

maestro – Extremely talented conductor, composer, musician, teacher, or in this case, chef.

Mare Tranquility – Mare is Latin for the word sea. The Sea of Tranquility was the landing site for the Apollo 11 lunar module which carried Buzz Aldrin and Neil Armstrong to the moon while Michael Collins remained in orbit, waiting to take them home. I remember when I was a kid, there was a female racehorse named Tranquility.

me bag – In the first grade, kids fill up a paper bag with things they like. The teacher opens one at a time and the other children guess which kid belongs to which bag.

mentor – Mentor was the teacher of Telemachus, son of Odysseus. Also, a tutor, teacher, guide, advisor.

Milky Way – The galaxy in which we humans live to eat candy bars by the same name manufactured by Mars.

mire – Muck.

MoMA – Museum of Modern Art.

Mrs. Grundy – A prudish, narrow minded, morally strict character in *Speed The Plough*, a play written by Thomas Morton in 1798. I can still recall Mrs. Grundy's comforting voice from my school days when, as a young lad, cast adrift in an unknown sea full of... moving along.

muck – Manure.

my cup of tea – Colloquial English expression meaning something you are fond of. In America, the expression is "my cup of joe."

oil and water – They do not mix very well and, in fact, can be extremely dangerous. When water is added to boiling oil, it will explode.

one man show – This very well could have been "a one woman show" but the masculine medial caesurae could not have preceded the word "a" and it would have thrown off the metric foot. Additionally, the word man is used as a non-gender specific modifier of the word "show" as in mankind. Anyway, male or female, "It's all about me."

Parthenon – A temple built on the Acropolis during the 5th century BCE to honor the Greek goddess, Athena.

peer – A duke, marquess, earl, viscount, or baron. A person's equal in terms of lifestyle, education, position, intellect...

people at the ballot box – Voters. People used to literally stuff small slips of paper in a box before the votes were tabulated. If they don't like you, they get rid of you.

Perry Mason – A fictional defense attorney created by Erle Stanley Gardner in the 1930s and popularized in novels, comic books, radio, and the long running TV show starring Raymond Burr.

physician – Doctor, doc, not to be confused with a very good basketball player named "J."

Picasso – (1881-1973) Pablo was a Spanish painter and founder of the "cubist" movement. He painted two versions of the well known, *Three Musicians.*

pinstripe suit – A suit with a vertical stripe. Bankers are sometimes referred to simply as "suits."

Poe – (1809-1849) Edgar Allen was an American author who wrote, *The Raven, Annabel Lee, The Tell-Tale Heart...*

Polaris – The North Star, the brightest star in the Little Dipper (Ursa Minor).

Pollock – (1912-1956) Jackson was an American artist whose work speaks for itself.

prescription – A directive by a doctor for some remedial action to be taken by a patient.

pundit – A person who gives his/her opinion in pop media, a commentator who is supposed to be an authority or expert in some particular area.

put you on your face – To faint.

put your feet to the fire – A practice, common in Shakespeare's England, whereby an unpopular politician's feet were heated up, not unlike a marshmallow or a wiener, to a very warm temperature. In order to cool them down, the politician must run as fast as he can, OUT OF TOWN.

quick columnists – Astute, bright, brilliant, clever, discriminating, intelligent, intuitive, knowledgeable, perceptive, sharp, and smart writers employed by a news organization.

River Seine – The romantic river that flows through the center of Paris.

sauté – To lightly fry in a pan with butter over high heat, usually associated with fine French cooking.

scratch – Chicken feed or money. It's good in golf. It's bad in pool. It used to be a bad thing to do to a record. Now it's good. It precedes "and sniff". It follows an itch. And it happened to the mare, Tranquility in the 6th at Belmont on June 1, 1963.

screech – Squeal, squawk, wail...the noise made by an owl and many of the contestants on the TV show "American Idol."

shower – A place to get wet and, hopefully, clean, also a place to sing.

soap box – A wooden container that holds soap, which, when inverted, can be used as a platform to stand on and preach. This practice, which continues to this day at Speaker's Corner in the north-east corner of Hyde Park in London, started in the late 1800s.

soufflé – A light dessert baked with eggs, originating in French kitchens, often topped with a sweet crème anglaise.

steel bars – Something behind which dishonest people are deposited.

stockholders – People who own shares in a company. Cowpokes are a different kind of stockholder. Tranquility's groom was a stockholder.

tack – A bridle and a saddle. These items make it easier to ride a horse and, presumably, a cow.

Taj Mahal – The mausoleum, marble dome, minarets, and surrounding structures built outside Agra, India by Emperor Shah Jahan to memorialize his third wife.

taunt – Tease, make fun of, heckle.

ten gallon hat – This is a really, really big hat. I mean, think of how big a fifty gallon drum is. Cowboys like Roy Rogers and John Wayne would presumably have worn one. I believe Eliza Doolittle wore one of these at Ascot.

The New York Times – The paper that really matters – if you are an author.

Theodor Geisel – (1904-1991) Dr. Seuss was a prolific American author of children's stories.

tough teens – bullies.

trash – Losses resulting from bad investments and fraud, garbage.

tuxedo – A dinner jacket worn at "black tie affairs." It can also be worn by the maitre d' of a fine restaurant.

'Twas – This is the opening word or two words in many great pieces of children's literature, second only to, Once upon a time.

Van Gogh – (1853-1890) Vincent was a Dutch painter known for his Self Portraits, *Potato Eaters*, *Sunflowers*, *Irises*, and *Starry Night*.

Versailles – Magnificent palace outside of Paris that contains the Hall of Mirrors, Louis XIV's royal residence and summer home of Napoleon. It is also the name of the town in Kentucky where the mare, Tranquility was raised.

Wall Street – A street in Manhattan where, in the 1700s, buyers and sellers of shares of stock would conduct business under a buttonwood tree.

wallow – Loll about like a pig in slop, cutting unsavory deals under the table.

was/were – In the 1500s Henry XVIII made the following statement, "If I were poor, I wouldn't be so fat." This was obviously incorrect. History showed Henry had a huge appetite. But I digress. It was also grammatically incorrect. Henry should have said, "If I was poor, I wouldn't be so fat." The court grammaticians, concerned that someone could loose a head over this error, quickly inserted a grammatical rule in the newly penned reference tome, *English For The English*. No copy of this book has ever been found, but through some diligent research, we believe we have distilled the essence of this particularly incongruous rule. Without going into great detail, it involved something about the past subjunctive of the verb "to be" when used with the first and third person singular subjective pronouns and whether or not the object was possible or impossible... It is all balderdash. We hereby request that the "experts" expunge this rule from all records. We believe this is what history has already done with Henry XVIII.

wiener – Weenie, hot dog, frankfurter, dog, brat, vienna sausage.

yodeled – The noise made by people in Austria and Switzerland looking for lost sheep.

you're supposed to reign supreme – You are the King or Queen of your own kingdom. The three biggest obstacles in your path on your journey to success are: #1 your own inability to dream of your success, #2 the naysayers who will inevitably try to convince you that success for you is not possible, and #3 The lack of ambition that drives you to work hard to achieve those dreams.

Dream it! Believe it! Work hard for it! Achieve it!